MW01178915

Thoughts, Emotions
&
Kindness

Facebook:
https://www.facebook.com/a.r.k.institute2020
Instagram: @d_ark_institute

Foreword

It's refreshing to encounter someone who puts caring, humility, concern, and tenderness at the forefront of every effort they take. Renée possesses an unquenching thirst to serve, not for glory or recognition, but to impact lives. This work is a testament to perseverance, authored by an introspective writer who applies the power of what she teaches. We are genuinely in awe of her courage to elevate and reimagine the possibilities of how many souls she can touch with her single message of helping others tap into the power of unwavering faith. As coaches, we are humbled to be recognized as an essential part of her self-discovery journey, as friends; we can personally attest that she is thoughtful, knowledgeable, and genuine. We urge you to be deliberate in meditating on every affirmation she penned because the sincerity will transform your mindset and manifest the incredible results you are envisioning.

Rio & Micca
Founders of POWERMATES

My Deepest Gratitude

This book came out of love.

I am profoundly grateful to my circle; my tribe as many would say. They saw the spark in me and gave me enough room to finally fly.

My parents, sister, brother in love, nephews and my family of many aunts, uncles, cousins, godchildren: thanks for you know how to keep me grounded and secure.

To my church family, Verity, I thank you for the many years of learning and to becoming a proud teacher and gift to stand bold in this Truth. Even my Sunday school kids, you all add to my smile.

To my core that allowed me to use my creative writing and empower countless others, the Dream Team, I am honoured.

To my photographer, Nickson Silva, you have a sharp eye!

To my creative and super talented designer, John W. Carter III, I am forever grateful for our paths crossing and for the bond that will never be broken.

And to my teachers, both here and those on their new assignment: I now see the view you were impressing in me. I may have kicked before, yet I stand confident now to continue the journey forward. I know you are with me. I got it. I will pass this on too.

Well hello journey seeker!

Pull up a pen and have an open mind. I am so glad that you picked up this journal! A.R.K. was a dream for many years but never realized until recently as the world was shifting. The more the world called out for help, the deeper the need became to make this dream become real. And here it is!

Kindness does not have to mean showing it outwardly to be recognized by others that social media has been promoting skewing the truth. While it is great to see it online, there is so much more to see offline as well. Kindness comes out of universal love of oneness. It is receiving someone's selflessness with a genuine sense of love and appreciation. It is in this moment; the recipient receives a sense of empowerment and hope while allowing their own light to shine before passing that gift forward. Think of it, as putting on a mask while on a turbulent plane. You must help yourself first. Otherwise, how can you help put on another's mask if you are passed out with no air?!

My hope and wish for you, is that you realize your greatest potential is deep within you. And it is needed now.

Now to use this journal is simple. I made it to be engaging. There will be moments to start in the morning and check in the evening. There will also be prompts to do something kind for someone. At the end of the day, ask yourself how you felt doing it. The goal is to check-in and monitor how you can **be** more, **do** more, and **have** more than you could have ever imagined!

As a wise teacher once said, "It works if you work it!" Allow the prompts to be your guide to self reflection and discover the hidden gem that needs to be showcased now. What are you looking to achieve? You must take time to do the work and start right now.

Remember, you are not in a race or a marathon with anyone though. This journal is for YOU. A combined set of days to grow, develop and finesse that Divine spark of yours into a radiant beam that attracts everything you desire! You are worthy! All that and a good bag of chips!

Be kind to yourself. Well, it is not too hard to find. Just look in the mirror, take a deep breath and smile. Tell yourself - I AM the light the world needs! I AM perfect, whole, and complete. I AM the link that my family, friends and even I need to survive.

So, as you take each day, know that I am walking with you. Each step, I have done and still doing. This is how I KNOW you can do it too. I BELIEVE in **you**.

Most of all, have FUN! I had a ball writing these in the early hours of the morning. I hope you enjoy the journal too.

Be radiant! Be glorious!

With the deepest sense of love,
Renée

This page is intentionally left blank. Let this spot be a reminder to start fresh. We are going to do this together. Write words, ideas or just remember that your mind is like a blank canvas that is ready to create anything you desire!

Day 1

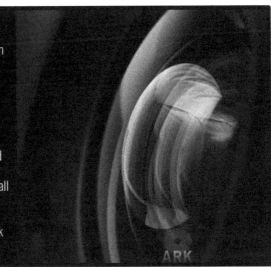

I am thankful for this day and for your grace to wake me up, Divine Spirit. I know all things are done in and through you. So, I ask for the activity of life to fill my body with good health. For universal love to bind me in your word and show compassion to others. That your Divine presence guides me with inspiration. The urge to act to bold step in and know I can do ALL things in your name and to claim all this as good because I am bountifully supplied with physical manifestations of everything I seek after.

ARK

What is my intention this day? How did I achieve today's goal?

_____

_____

_____

_____

_____

_____

_____

_____

Day 2

I say a prayer for the world this morning. That the anointing grace of our Heavenly Spirit pour grace into this universe. That each soul, animal, tree or living thing find comfort in a time that is somewhat turbulent.

May the light of love shine through each dark space and illumine that which is good, noble and true. Today, I hold steadfast that it is love that makes the world go round. And it begins with me to see it in every moment, person or thought throughout the day.

So I pray for the healing balm to bind, cement and hold the voids together as the earth reboots.

Who are your top five people that you want to see succeed? Why did you choose them?

Day 3

Thank you Divine Spirit for I am always at work, for your glory. Yet today, I allow myself to play. To be child-like and fellowship with others in a spirit of love and joy. My hope is that our bond will make us stronger not just in deed but in a youthful expression of who and what you represent in us. All is well. Amen.

What 3 things are you grateful for today?

_____

_____

_____

_____

_____

_____

_____

_____

Day 4

Thank you for being the Master craftsman that has molded me and shaped my life; the design of what I am today.

As you sculpt me, I am filled with gifts, complete ideas and talents to share my beauty and love with this world.

Have Thy own way.

Look in the mirror in the morning and the evening for 30 seconds. Who do you see looking back at you? Get specific; love, hurt, a soul bursting.

Day 5

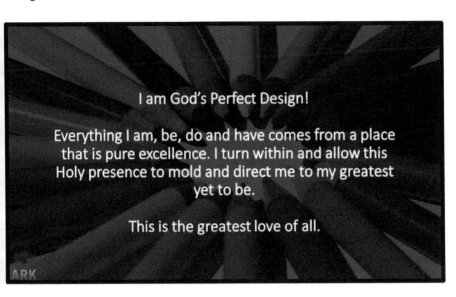

What is one of your hidden talents that you have not shared with the world yet? Why? If you did, what do you think others would say?

Day 6

*What are 3 things that makes you beautiful, bold,
dynamic and unrepeatable? I challenge you to jot
down more! Sit and honour yourself. You are magic!*

Day 7

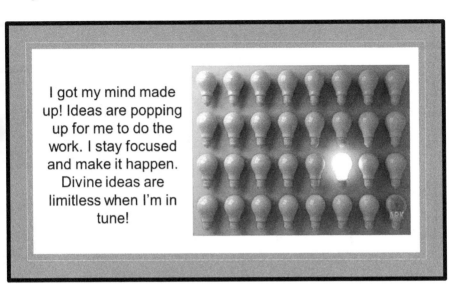

I got my mind made up! Ideas are popping up for me to do the work. I stay focused and make it happen. Divine ideas are limitless when I'm in tune!

List 5 new things about yourself that you discovered recently. Can one of these become a new hobby or business?

_____

_____

_____

_____

_____

_____

_____

Day 8

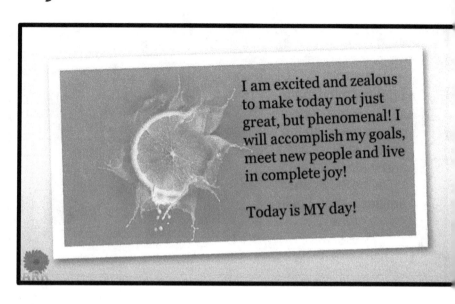

I am excited and zealous to make today not just great, but phenomenal! I will accomplish my goals, meet new people and live in complete joy!

Today is MY day!

What are you excited about today? How BIG is this idea or dream? Spend time daydreaming around it. Let inspiration move you!

Day 9

How sweet it is to be loved by you, heavenly Spirit. You continue to pour into me all that I need to be, do and have to overflow! I love you above all else for you give me life! You are my peace and I long to serve you.

ARK

What 5 things do you love about yourself? About the world? Can any of these become part of your pay it forward stance?

Day 10

Divine Spirit, wash away my iniquities
that is not of your love. Release me
from my negative thoughts and feelings
for it is blocking me from my highest
and best good. I now claim my birthright
as your blessed child, abundantly
supplied and filled with your grace.
All is well.

What or who do you need to forgive? What's holding you back from you being radiant?! Write a note of things to let go and at the end burn it. How do you feel now?

Day 11

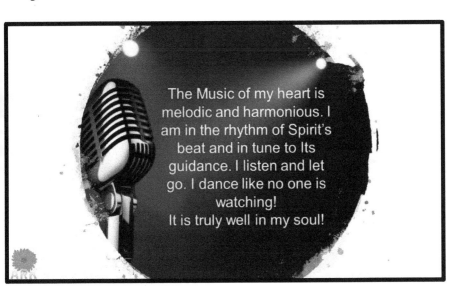

The Music of my heart is melodic and harmonious. I am in the rhythm of Spirit's beat and in tune to Its guidance. I listen and let go. I dance like no one is watching!
It is truly well in my soul!

List 4 songs that make you dance. Throughout the day, play them and pay attention to how you feel. Describe it in your writing tonight.

_____

_____

_____

_____

_____

_____

_____

Day 12

In the stillness, I am at peace. I tune into that calmness, the guided wisdom and turn off the outside noise. I seek to be better in these moments than the past. I thank you sweet Spirit for life.

Take 5 minutes and just breathe. Sit. Inhale. Exhale. Repeat. Now, write what came up for you.

_____

_____

_____

_____

_____

_____

_____

Day 13

Hope springs eternal. Therefore, I am a vessel of hope, excited today to know that everything I seek, is now mine by Divine consciousness. All that I need is here, now being made manifest because my indwelling Source knows the things that I need; even before I utter a word. So, I just say Thank you!

What are 5 steps that you can take towards fulfilling your dreams.

Day 14

I am at the banquet table of abundance. I am blessed beyond measure. Everything I need to be nourished is before me. I need not hoard for there is plenty now and forever. I joyfully receive the abundance that is mine!
Amen.

Mindful eating time! Pick 3 days and eat without any electronic device on or at hand. What did you notice?

Day 15

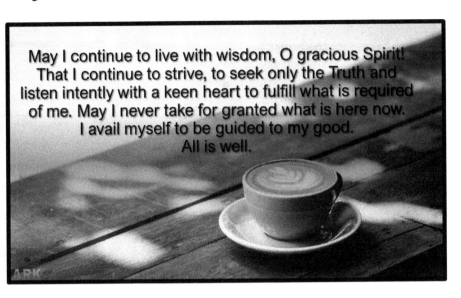

May I continue to live with wisdom, O gracious Spirit!
That I continue to strive, to seek only the Truth and
listen intently with a keen heart to fulfill what is required
of me. May I never take for granted what is here now.
I avail myself to be guided to my good.
All is well.

List 20 new things that you are grateful for about YOU! ie. Your hair, smile, toes, hands. (You get the idea.)

_____

_____

_____

_____

_____

_____

_____

Day 16

I give thanks for the nudge to wake up this day. I am awake, alive and alert to be the best me in this now moment. I am a Divine light of Truth. All that Spirit is, I am that and so much more. I creatively, lovingly and wisely let my light shine to draw out the best of me and attract others of same likeness. WE will be magnificent together. I know all is well. And so it is.

Create a new habit around your sleep. Try going to bed 30 minutes earlier. How did that feel?

Day 17

I have a feeling or urge that cannot be suppressed. My dreams and thoughts ponder what it is. Who do I turn to for the answer? And then I hear a soft whisper that says, "Follow me." And with no hesitation, I turn inward to that indwelling presence of Divine Spirit that gives me a boost to be guided to my gifts and talents. I turn and release the Divine potential within me, and I am set free. The vision over my life has made me whole. Thank you, Spirit!

Create a vision board with only positive words. Place it where you can see and focus on it for the remaining of your journal days. What came up for you?

Day 18

I am a leader! I am a conqueror! I can do all things through the indwelling Christ that strengthens me. Therefore, I am made to stand out in this world. I am a true light for all to see. Today is my day!

Describe yourself in 5 words. Why did you choose those exact words? Post your words on your bathroom mirror and use it to remind yourself how great you are!

Day 19

I am rich in favour and flavour! That my gift or talent adds a light in this world. I am unique with my talent and give freely as the world receives. Just like a coffee bean, I am rich and good to the last drop! I am what the world needs today and everyday.

Describe what a perfect day would look like from sunrise to sunset? Don't rush this activity. Also notice and write down what you feel.

Day 20

I am the spark of life that adds to this world! That my presence is beautiful! I am a unique flower in the garden of life! As I continue to unfold into my greatest self, I am sending out that scent of love, joy and peace to all.

ARA

Give cards of affirmations to 5 youths. It does not have to be family ties. Make it unique to them. How did you feel? How did they feel? What was their reaction?

Day 21

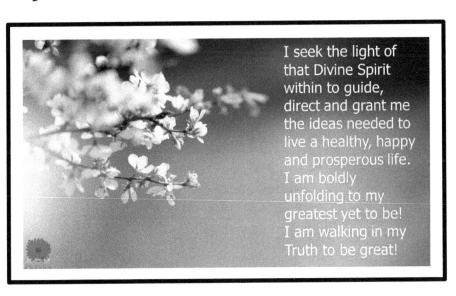

I seek the light of that Divine Spirit within to guide, direct and grant me the ideas needed to live a healthy, happy and prosperous life. I am boldly unfolding to my greatest yet to be! I am walking in my Truth to be great!

Pick something off your dream list and do it! Note your feelings. Remember, the more you give something back to yourself, the stronger you are to overcome anything!

> Today, I release thoughts and feelings
> that aren't quite up to par. Expectations
> that I placed on myself or of others and I
> now declare that I am free. I've done
> nothing wrong as it was based on my old
> perception of self yesterday.
> This new day, I bring forth joy, a focused
> heart and openness to be guided by
> Spirit. It is done. And so it is.

Write two letters. One of all the things you are letting go. Burn that. The other, make it a love note to yourself. Keep it and read it in 6 months.

Day 23

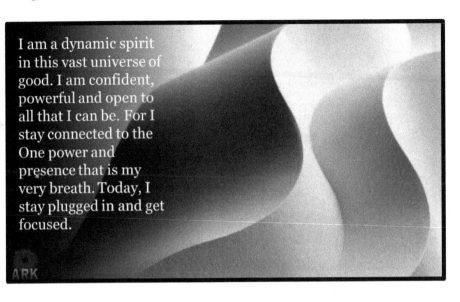

I am a dynamic spirit in this vast universe of good. I am confident, powerful and open to all that I can be. For I stay connected to the One power and presence that is my very breath. Today, I stay plugged in and get focused.

ARK

Pick a location or community project and serve for a day. Do it for your own soul's liberation. Journal the experience.

_____

_____

_____

_____

_____

_____

_____

Day 24

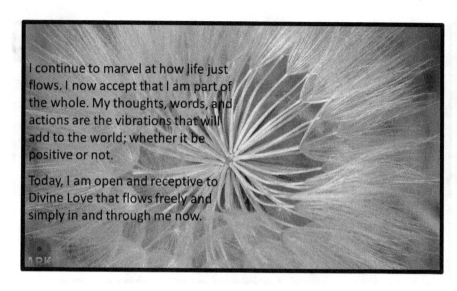

I continue to marvel at how life just flows. I now accept that I am part of the whole. My thoughts, words, and actions are the vibrations that will add to the world; whether it be positive or not.

Today, I am open and receptive to Divine Love that flows freely and simply in and through me now.

What are you open to doing or receiving today?
What did you accept and manifest?

Day 25

I am one with Divine Spirit. I am one with all people. I am one with all life.

I am thankful that each moment of the day provides me with an opportunity to be, do or have something that I desire. I am limitless!

ARK

An evening of self care is in order! What did you do? How did you feel?

Day 26

O Sweet Spirit, I thank you for this day! I am here to be a loving and supportive light for others. To give freely as I have received. As this day is a day to remember those with disabilities, may I be mindful that we all have something to release. To dis-able is to no longer hold that I am limited or limiting another to grow and prosper. That the real work is within me, us, and it is time to love. Love with our whole self.

How can you level up your spiritual routine? Devote 10 more minutes to taking time to meditate and reflect on your insights.

Day 27

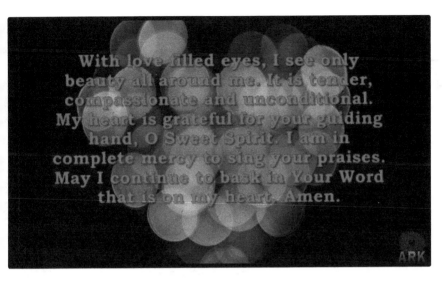

With love filled eyes, I see only beauty all around me. It is tender, compassionate and unconditional. My heart is grateful for your guiding hand, O Sweet Spirit. I am in complete mercy to sing your praises. May I continue to bask in Your Word that is on my heart. Amen.

ARK

Pay it forward. Write a letter and tell someone you know how much you appreciate them. A thank you gesture has a long-lasting effect!

_____

_____

_____

_____

_____

_____

_____

Day 28

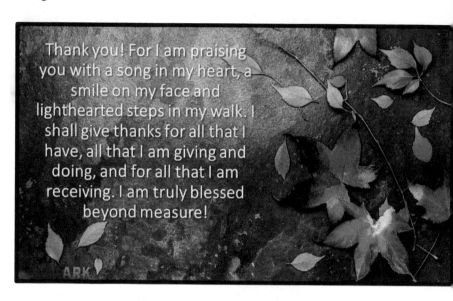

Thank you! For I am praising you with a song in my heart, a smile on my face and lighthearted steps in my walk. I shall give thanks for all that I have, all that I am giving and doing, and for all that I am receiving. I am truly blessed beyond measure!

ARK

Name 15 ways to thank yourself for being awesome this morning! Now write 10 more tonight. Any similarities?

Day 29

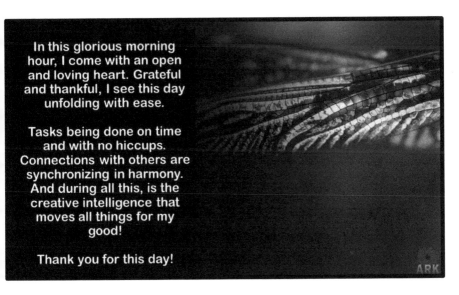

In this glorious morning hour, I come with an open and loving heart. Grateful and thankful, I see this day unfolding with ease.

Tasks being done on time and with no hiccups. Connections with others are synchronizing in harmony. And during all this, is the creative intelligence that moves all things for my good!

Thank you for this day!

ARK

Catch either a sunrise or sunset. Just watch nature and journal your thoughts.

_____

_____

_____

_____

_____

_____

_____

_____

Day 30

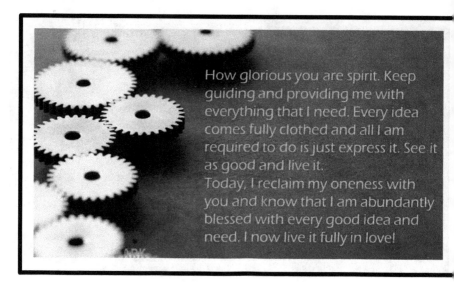

How glorious you are spirit. Keep guiding and providing me with everything that I need. Every idea comes fully clothed and all I am required to do is just express it. See it as good and live it.
Today, I reclaim my oneness with you and know that I am abundantly blessed with every good idea and need. I now live it fully in love!

Name a small change that can make you a better person today and for the next 10 days.

Day 31

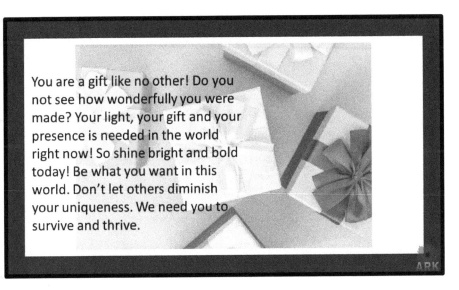

You are a gift like no other! Do you not see how wonderfully you were made? Your light, your gift and your presence is needed in the world right now! So shine bright and bold today! Be what you want in this world. Don't let others diminish your uniqueness. We need you to survive and thrive.

List your gifts and talents. Now take 5 and share it with a young person. Become a leader the world needs!

Day 32

I am poised and laser focused on my goals. There is a sense of ease and calm as I go about my day. All is well.

No criticism zone. For the rest of the day, you will not hold a negative thought about yourself. If one tries to overwhelm you, let it go and jot down how many times one appeared. Less than 15, good; 10 is awesome; 5 is wonderful!

Day 33

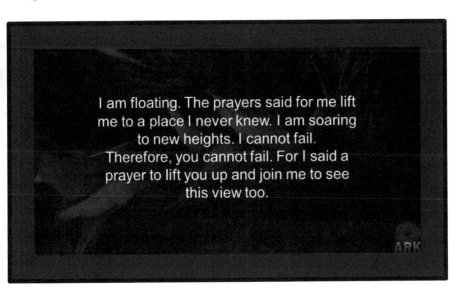

I am floating. The prayers said for me lift me to a place I never knew. I am soaring to new heights. I cannot fail. Therefore, you cannot fail. For I said a prayer to lift you up and join me to see this view too.

ARK

For the next 7 days, write a positive affirmation for 3 others in your circle in your journal. Record what transpires with them. Note how you feel too.

Day 34

I take time to just pause and say thank you. For truly I am not alone in this world. There are others who are with me; seeking to be their best self. And now, I see the beauty of life.

What are 3 ways that you can support your inner circle? Do something unexpected and reflect.

Day 35

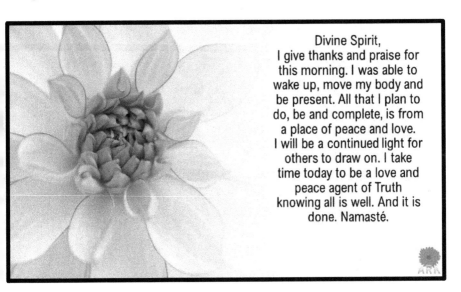

Divine Spirit,
I give thanks and praise for this morning. I was able to wake up, move my body and be present. All that I plan to do, be and complete, is from a place of peace and love. I will be a continued light for others to draw on. I take time today to be a love and peace agent of Truth knowing all is well. And it is done. Namasté.

What makes you smile? List 25 things and then, smile.

Day 36

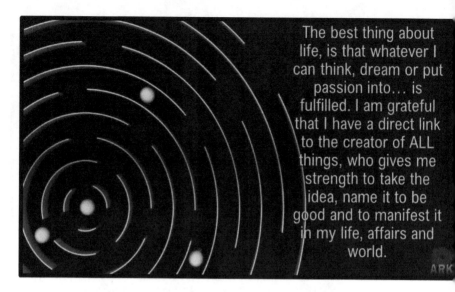

The best thing about life, is that whatever I can think, dream or put passion into... is fulfilled. I am grateful that I have a direct link to the creator of ALL things, who gives me strength to take the idea, name it to be good and to manifest it in my life, affairs and world.

ARK

What positive things have happened since you started this 90-day journal. List them all!

Day 37

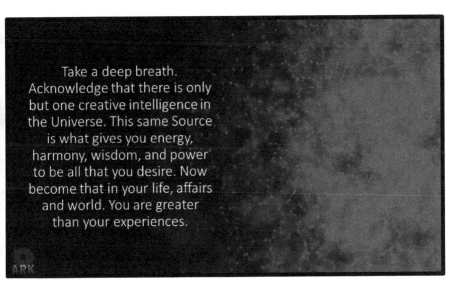

Take a deep breath. Acknowledge that there is only but one creative intelligence in the Universe. This same Source is what gives you energy, harmony, wisdom, and power to be all that you desire. Now become that in your life, affairs and world. You are greater than your experiences.

Do a 15 minute deep breathing exercise. How did it feel to just breathe from your diaphragm?

_____

_____

_____

_____

_____

_____

_____

_____

Day 38

I am life.
I am love.
I am peace.
I am the light that
attracts, harmonizes
and unifies with all.
I am grateful.
All is well.
And so it is.

Write another 10 I Am statements that are authentic to you.

_____

_____

_____

_____

_____

_____

_____

Day 39

Life is for living and I
am living it with zeal
and love!

I will use this day to
create, to produce and
to enjoy all that Spirit
has placed in me. I am
one with my indwelling
Christ.

And so it is.

Adventure day! Go out and have fun. Dance, play or catch up with a friend. Just be excited and journal!

_____

_____

_____

_____

_____

_____

_____

Day 40

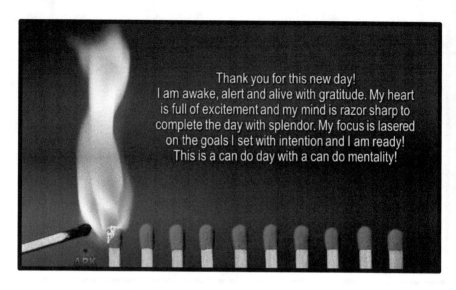

Thank you for this new day!
I am awake, alert and alive with gratitude. My heart
is full of excitement and my mind is razor sharp to
complete the day with splendor. My focus is lasered
on the goals I set with intention and I am ready!
This is a can do day with a can do mentality!

What are your 3 goals for this day? Name and claim them done!

_____

_____

_____

_____

_____

_____

_____

_____

Day 41

I am walking in Truth. I am no longer being limited by what others say I can or cannot do. I trust my own intuition to create, design and masterfully manifest in my life, affairs and world. I am limitless! I am free!

What are you looking to let go? Write them down and then hold a burning bowl ceremony. When you release it, write new statements that you desire.

_____

_____

_____

_____

_____

_____

_____

Day 42

This day is mine to discover! I am excited in what I can do, try and become! I am finding hidden gems in myself that is amazing! Everything is available to me, right here and now!

ARK

What 3 new things did you learn about yourself today?

_____

_____

_____

_____

_____

_____

_____

_____

Day 43

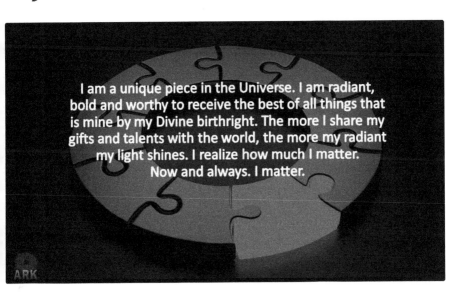

I am a unique piece in the Universe. I am radiant, bold and worthy to receive the best of all things that is mine by my Divine birthright. The more I share my gifts and talents with the world, the more my radiant my light shines. I realize how much I matter. Now and always. I matter.

ARK

What do you want to manifest into your life NOW? A new romance? A career change? A new skill or hobby?

Day 44

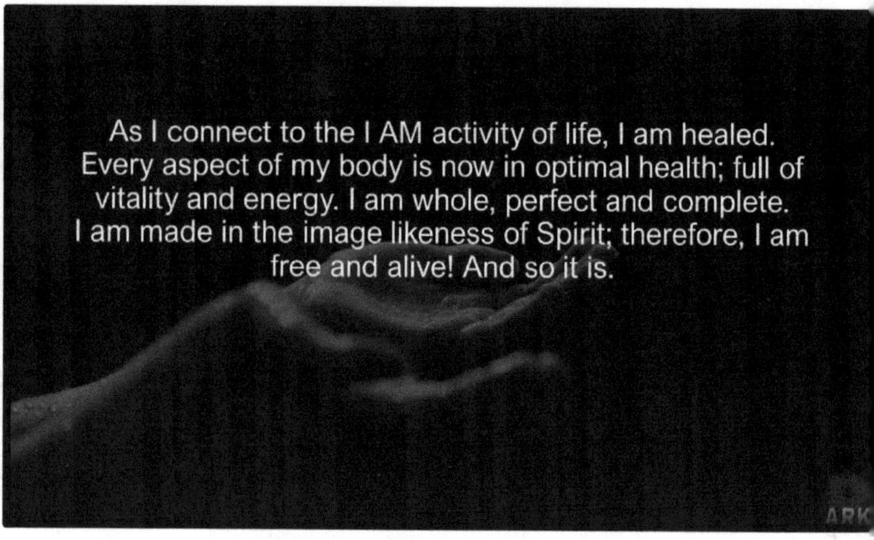

What was one of your favourite moments during this process that you can't stop smiling about?

_____

_____

_____

_____

_____

_____

_____

Day 45

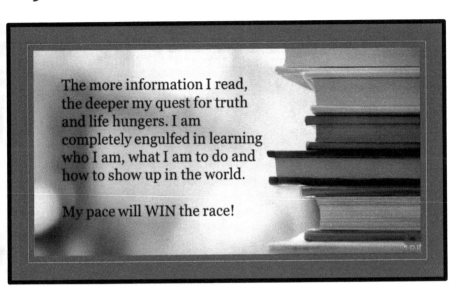

The more information I read, the deeper my quest for truth and life hungers. I am completely engulfed in learning who I am, what I am to do and how to show up in the world.

My pace will WIN the race!

Find 3 new books that feed your drive for success or self discovery.

_____

_____

_____

_____

_____

_____

_____

_____

Day 46

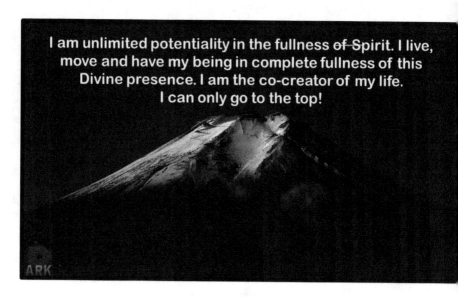

I am unlimited potentiality in the fullness of Spirit. I live, move and have my being in complete fullness of this Divine presence. I am the co-creator of my life. I can only go to the top!

ARK

What do you think it means to be a co-creator?
What are you a co-creator of right now in your life?

Day 47

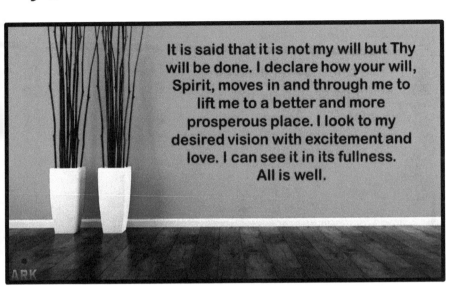

It is said that it is not my will but Thy will be done. I declare how your will, Spirit, moves in and through me to lift me to a better and more prosperous place. I look to my desired vision with excitement and love. I can see it in its fullness. All is well.

What are you willing to let go emotionally? What can you add to your new love language instead?

Day 48

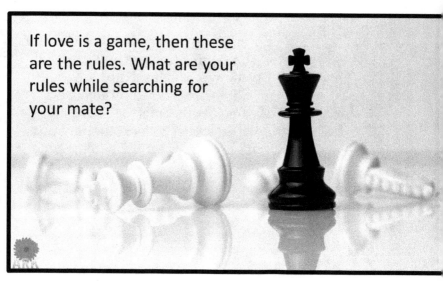

If love is a game, then these are the rules. What are your rules while searching for your mate?

Write a list of qualities that you desire in a romantic interest or of yourself. Note that the more you show self love, the greater you find harmony around you.

Day 49

I am motivated this day to make new connections! To meet new people, be open to new ideas and express kindness everywhere I go!

Good morning Kings & Queens!

Make 3 new acquaintances in your personal or professional world.

Day 50

The beauty within me now radiates from a place of divine peace and love. I am that essence of grace, joy and harmony. Today, I choose to be the best expression of beauty that I can be. Whether in words, thoughts or deeds, I will create from a place of complete spiritual understanding. I choose this day to be love in action! Good morning!

What do you love about yourself? Why? Journal how you can have monthly self love moments and schedule them on your calendar.

Day 51

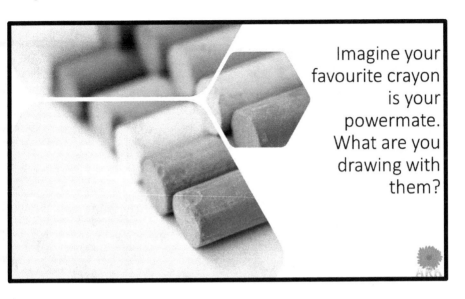

Imagine your favourite crayon is your powermate. What are you drawing with them?

What is your best attribute? Hands? Smile? Eyes? What about the person you are attracted to? What do they see in you?

_____

_____

_____

_____

_____

_____

_____

Day 52

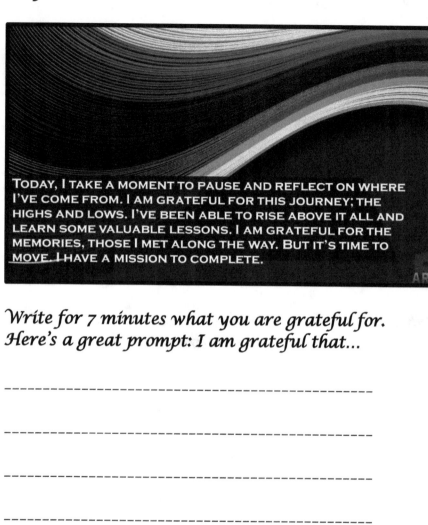

TODAY, I TAKE A MOMENT TO PAUSE AND REFLECT ON WHERE I'VE COME FROM. I AM GRATEFUL FOR THIS JOURNEY; THE HIGHS AND LOWS. I'VE BEEN ABLE TO RISE ABOVE IT ALL AND LEARN SOME VALUABLE LESSONS. I AM GRATEFUL FOR THE MEMORIES, THOSE I MET ALONG THE WAY. BUT IT'S TIME TO MOVE. I HAVE A MISSION TO COMPLETE.

ARK

Write for 7 minutes what you are grateful for.
Here's a great prompt: I am grateful that...

Day 53

YOU are an unrepeatable, unique gift to this world. Never forget to stand out from the crowd!

Look in the mirror. Write 7 things that you like about yourself?

Day 54

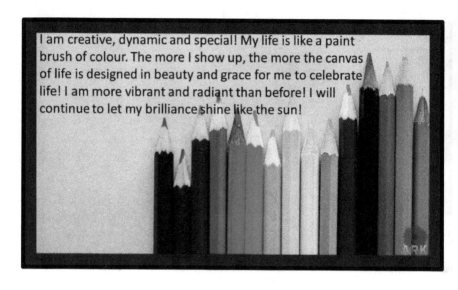

I am creative, dynamic and special! My life is like a paint brush of colour. The more I show up, the more the canvas of life is designed in beauty and grace for me to celebrate life! I am more vibrant and radiant than before! I will continue to let my brilliance shine like the sun!

Create a routine that boosts your confidence and complete 3 key tasks today!

_____

_____

_____

_____

_____

_____

_____

Day 55

I am rejuvenated and ready for today! I am sending vibrations of **POWER** to my friends, loved ones and the world. I connect with those who are seeking me with the same intensity!
Be encouraged!

Create 3 new healthy goals. Get excited. Take action by writing them down and track your results.

Day 56

Today I am excited to step into
this day ready to paint my world
with vibrant colours! Each
intention allows me to create a
world filled with love and light! I
am open to this process and will
listen to Divine Guidance.

All is well!

Find something creative to do for 30 minutes. Have fun!

Day 57

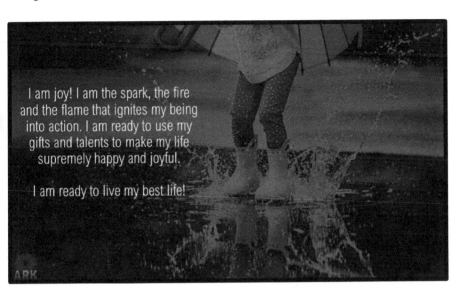

I am joy! I am the spark, the fire and the flame that ignites my being into action. I am ready to use my gifts and talents to make my life supremely happy and joyful.

I am ready to live my best life!

ARK

What are 5 things that make you smile. Choose one and incorporate that into today's routine.

Day 58

Life is always playing a song. No matter the tempo, I move to Its rhythm. I am in sync with the cords and sway with the harmony. It is in me and I in it. There is no separation. So I keep on dancing like no one is watching.

Create an upbeat playlist. Play it throughout the day and record how the whole day went. Bonus if you can do it for a week!

Day 59

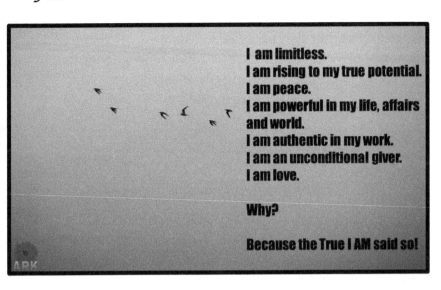

I am limitless.
I am rising to my true potential.
I am peace.
I am powerful in my life, affairs and world.
I am authentic in my work.
I am an unconditional giver.
I am love.

Why?

Because the True I AM said so!

What is your greatest strength? Why did you choose that particular asset?

Day 60

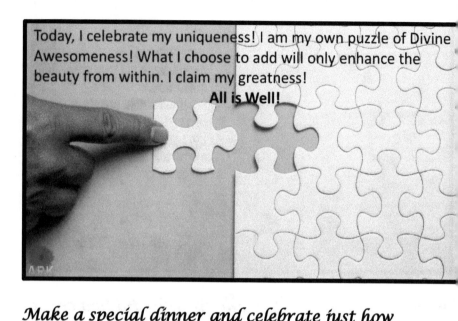

Today, I celebrate my uniqueness! I am my own puzzle of Divine Awesomeness! What I choose to add will only enhance the beauty from within. I claim my greatness!
All is Well!

Make a special dinner and celebrate just how amazing you are. Get dressed up, set the mood, and breathe. You are worthy!

Day 61

I am grateful for a day manifesting harmony with others! I dreamt of a peaceful day and I received it!

What do you want to learn more about in your self discovery time? Writing? Reading? The Art of Breathing?

Day 62

I am renewed, revitalized and refocused in the goodness of Spirit. I am made in the image-likeness of the Divine! Be made brand new from within! Rise to your greatest potential! Shine like the sun! Shine your light!

How do you destress? Create a list to share with others.

Day 63

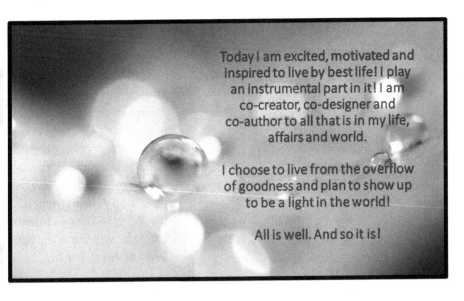

Today I am excited, motivated and inspired to live by best life! I play an instrumental part in it! I am co-creator, co-designer and co-author to all that is in my life, affairs and world.

I choose to live from the overflow of goodness and plan to show up to be a light in the world!

All is well. And so it is!

What's your favourite song? When did you hear it last? Play it now and just dance!

_____

_____

_____

_____

_____

_____

_____

_____

Day 64

I stand in the acknowledgment that I am the light that is needed to shine! The fact that I step into my truth, everything falls into place. The right people, place and opportunities appear. I am the light that adds to the world! Everything is working in Divine Order! Today, I will shine my light and stand in Truth!

Light a candle and just have 20 minutes of quiet. Journal.

Day 65

So what are you planting in your land of imagination? The best time to plant is now!

Buy a plant and for the next 21 days, speak affirmations to it. How is it responding to you?

_____

_____

_____

_____

_____

_____

_____

Thank you for the many
blessings... for my home,
work and life!
My home is built on Your
Word. Each command placed
in me, will not just grow but
thrive. May I continue to
build a solid foundation with
the Truth and live-in
harmony and peace.
And so it is.

Take a look at your home surroundings. Speak a
blessing or a positive phrase over everything.
Example, I thank you sofa for the comfy snuggles.

Day 67

I am love! I am joy! I am peace! I am wise! I am all that positive, great stuff that Divine Spirit is! I am grateful for everyone and everything in my life, my affairs and my world!

Today I choose love.

Grand loving morning!

I love you!

Look in the mirror. What 7 things do you love about what you see?

_____

_____

_____

_____

_____

_____

_____

_____

Day 68

Today, I rise with commitment to my inner guide, that I will show up and say yes! I will commit to being a loving magnet and a giver of life to the world!
All is perfect and complete!

Mindfulness moment. Take 1 meal today and enjoy it without social media or technology. Journal your findings.

Day 69

I am a glorious and vibrant light that shines brightly. I am tranquil, peaceful and loving. Today, I allow all that is in me to flow freely with my imagination and claim my dreams right here and now. Good morning!

What is 3 unique things about yourself that no one would know? Share it with someone special to you.

I am calm, poised and purposeful. I am eager to meet today with a smile on my face and joy in my heart. I see everything working in my life with ease and tranquility. Today, I use my gift of wisdom to guide me towards my goals. All is well.

Take 15 minutes and listen to something relaxing. Journal how you felt afterwards.

Day 71

I am open and receptive.
Spirit, use me as an instrument to draw what my imagination has envisioned.
Absolute good is mine now!

I claim it and all is well.

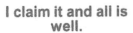

Try a new hobby or activity today? How did it feel to stretch your comfort zone?

_____

_____

_____

_____

_____

_____

_____

_____

Day 72

I am delighted that I came to WIN big! I am thankful for I give freely in love to others. My work and gifts are being received in love and grace!

Thank you Divine Spirit! All is well!

Pay it forward time! Write 10 sentences in cards and give to anyone? How did they react? How did you feel?

Day 73

I recognize that compassion is the order for today. What I know to be true is that my vibration of care, kindness and agape love is being sent out. Virtual hugs and smiles will be received and return to me 100-fold!

Good morning!

Pay it forward today: Do something kind for someone without seeking recognition? How did you feel? How did they react?

_____

_____

_____

_____

_____

_____

_____

Day 74

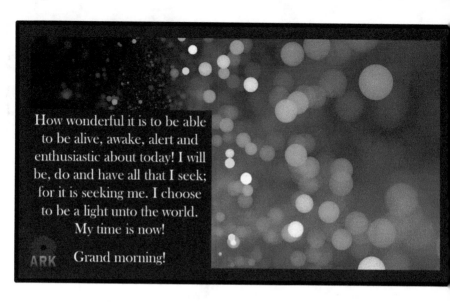

How wonderful it is to be able to be alive, awake, alert and enthusiastic about today! I will be, do and have all that I seek; for it is seeking me. I choose to be a light unto the world. My time is now!

ARK   Grand morning!

What are you thankful for about yourself? Write all that you can until you can't stop!

_____

_____

_____

_____

_____

_____

_____

_____

Day 75

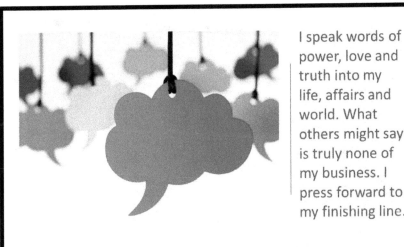

I speak words of power, love and truth into my life, affairs and world. What others might say is truly none of my business. I press forward to my finishing line.

What 10 things are you most proud of about yourself? More than 10, great!

_____

_____

_____

_____

_____

_____

_____

_____

Day 76

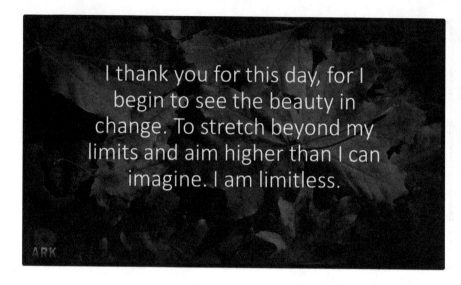

I thank you for this day, for I begin to see the beauty in change. To stretch beyond my limits and aim higher than I can imagine. I am limitless.

ARK

What are you motivated to do this day? How will you stay focused on making it a successful win before bedtime?

Day 77

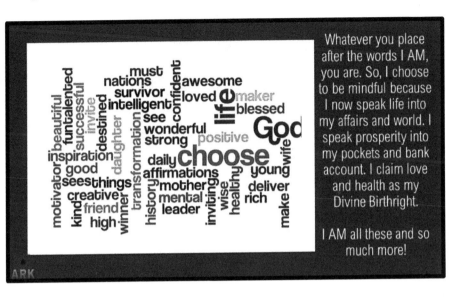

Positive Word Switch! Create a board of positive words using every letter of the alphabet! Be creative!

_____

_____

_____

_____

_____

_____

_____

Day 78

I keep watch over my thoughts and feelings. I stand on Truth. Today, I ensure that my words, feelings, actions and reactions are in alignment with Spirit. What I think on today, has a direct connection to the outer. I work and give in love; knowing it will prosper me.

What is my vision for the next 3 years? Take time to reflect on the goal. Then break it into smaller tasks and finally set a time frame to accomplish each. I know you will manifest this and something bigger!

Day 79

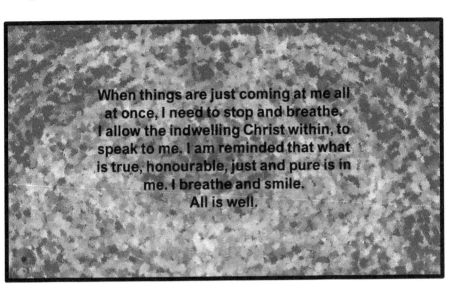

When things are just coming at me all
at once, I need to stop and breathe.
I allow the indwelling Christ within, to
speak to me. I am reminded that what
is true, honourable, just and pure is in
me. I breathe and smile.
All is well.

Go for a walk. Take in the surroundings of nature and breathe. Then, write what came to mind. Bonus to take a photo and visit it when you need a boost.

Day 80

I am renewed, enlightened and ready to share my gift with the world! I am prosperous!

When was the last time you took a self care me day? This week? Last week? A month ago? A year or more? Make that happen today!

_____

_____

_____

_____

_____

_____

_____

Day 81

I am rich in favour and flavour! My gifts or talents adds to this world. I am unique and give freely as the world receives. Just like a coffee bean, I am rich and good to the last drop! I am what the world needs today and everyday.

What motivates you? What colour inspires your mood? Wear it today and stay in the flow of love!

_____

_____

_____

_____

_____

_____

_____

_____

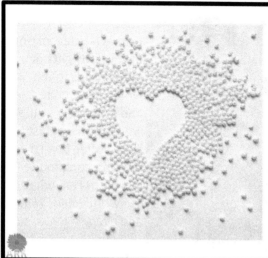

Another new day is dawning! I am thankful and encouraged to connect with those on the path to seeking Truth. For the road may be lonely but this isn't for the weak. I send out words of empowerment, support and joy to my mate – I wish you a phenomenal day of productivity! I send out wishes to my likeminded journey dwellers too!

What accomplishment are you most proud of? Why that one? How can you expand that feeling on a regular basis?

Day 83

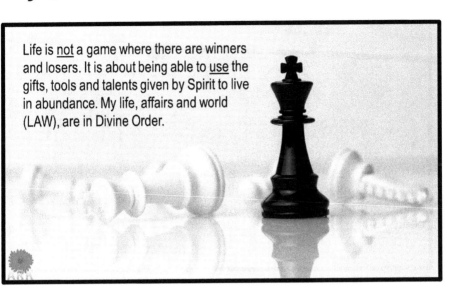

Life is __not__ a game where there are winners and losers. It is about being able to __use__ the gifts, tools and talents given by Spirit to live in abundance. My life, affairs and world (LAW), are in Divine Order.

Life is about taking chances and living? What are you taking the leap of faith on? Do not contemplate this. Do it!

_____

_____

_____

_____

_____

_____

_____

Day 84

Joy is in the eye of the beholder! So, I behold the beauty, joy, and love in you! You are magnificent, charismatic and a delight! You are the sunshine the world needs. Shine on!

What brings you joy in your life, affairs, and world? How can you express more of that to your daily routine?

Day 85

The best part of life's journey is knowing that I do not walk alone. I am guided, sustained and loved by the fullness of Spirit. Peace be still.

ARK

Do you have an accountability person or team? Why not? If yes, then what do they support you with?

_____

_____

_____

_____

_____

_____

_____

Day 86

Today, I stand basking in the sun realizing that I am one with all life! Everything, even the smallest particle in the universe is sending me the energy needed to be my greatest self! I receive and give with gratitude!

What brings you peace? What made you smile today?

_____

_____

_____

_____

_____

_____

_____

_____

Day 87

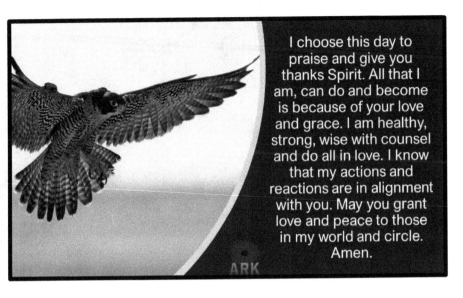

I choose this day to praise and give you thanks Spirit. All that I am, can do and become is because of your love and grace. I am healthy, strong, wise with counsel and do all in love. I know that my actions and reactions are in alignment with you. May you grant love and peace to those in my world and circle. Amen.

What is on your mind right now? What do you feel about yourself?

Day 88

There is a time to bloom, a time to plant and a time to harvest. I am in the season of clearing the area out to start planting for the newness that is coming! I am ready for my season of plenty and abundance.

ARK

What seedling or idea are you going to plant about yourself? Physically, plant a seed, name it and watch it and yourself grow into something special.

_____

_____

_____

_____

_____

_____

_____

Day 89

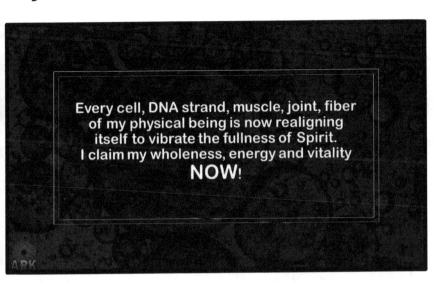

Every cell, DNA strand, muscle, joint, fiber
of my physical being is now realigning
itself to vibrate the fullness of Spirit.
I claim my wholeness, energy and vitality
NOW!

Do you see yourself healthy? If not, what 3 things can you do now to make a positive change? Sleep? Healthy eating? More exercise?

Day 90

Sweet Spirit, may I continue to lean on you for wisdom, strength and support. May this day be a reminder that I cannot be silent on the injustices of the world when I see it. Everyone is part of the whole and I need them to survive. Their gifts, words or light, adds to mine and we are powerful together. Today, I stand for love, justice and peace.
May everyone find comfort in you today, for you will always make a way.
Amen.

Write 10 new goals that you plan to take ACTION on today. Be YOU! You made it!

Join the Community!

Please know there is a Facebook page that you can join. You can share your wins, ask questions, and find some amazing tools that can assist you in living your best life now!

You can be part of the kindness family by going to, https://www.facebook.com/a.r.k.institute2020. If you need some time and privacy, then you are welcome to send me an email at d.arkinstitute2020@gmail.com.

Know you are not alone in this journey. It's one of the reasons I jumped into this year and decided to shine my light. I am committed to finding ways to uplift and empower anyone that I cross paths with.

I am super grateful that you took the journey to love yourself. You are deserving of love; first from within, then without.

I believe in you. I have faith that you are a winner beyond your wildest dream or thought. Never give up. And truly, I love you for the beauty that you are! Congratulations for completing the 90-day journey for you!

~ Renée